Nibbling the Page

Poems in Different Forms

selected by Wes Magee
illustrated by Sarah Geeves
and Sue Woollatt

LONGMAN

Contents

Me and Amanda

Me and
Amanda
meander
like rivers
that run to
the sea. We
wander at
random,
we're
always in
tandem,
meandering
Mandy and
me.

Colin West

Roger the Dog

Asleep he wheezes at his ease.
He only wakes to scratch his fleas.

He hogs the fire, he bakes his head
As if it were a loaf of bread.

He's just a sack of snoring dog.
You can lug him like a log.

You can roll him with your foot,
He'll stay snoring where he's put.

I take him out for exercise,
He rolls in cowclap up to his eyes.

He will not race, he will not romp,
He saves his strength for gobble and chomp.

He'll work as hard as you could wish
Emptying his dinner dish,

Then flops flat, and digs down deep,
Like a miner, into sleep.

Ted Hughes

What the Wind Said

Where to Wind? Where to?
Round the chimneys, down the flue.

After that? What after that?
Going to spin off someone's hat.

Where will that be? Tell us where?
In the centre of town square.

Whose hat is it? Tell us who?
Mrs Hoity-Toity Fortescue.

Where to then? Where to then?
Chasing mist across the fen.

Which way, Wind? Now which way?
Over the fields and miles away.

Matt Simpson

Grandad

Grandad's dead
And I'm sorry about that.

He'd a huge black overcoat.
He felt proud in it.
You could have hidden
A football crowd in it.
Far too big –
It was a lousy fit
But Grandad didn't mind a bit.
He wore it all winter
With a squashed black hat.

Now he's dead
And I'm sorry about that.

He'd got twelve stories.
I'd heard every one of them
Hundreds of times
But that was the fun of them:
You knew what was coming
So you could join in.
He'd got big hands
And brown, grooved skin
And when he laughed
It knocked you flat.

Now he's dead
And I'm sorry about that.   **Kit Wright**

There Was a Young Farmer of Leeds

There was a young farmer of Leeds
Who swallowed six packets of seeds,
    It soon came to pass
    He was covered with grass,
And he couldn't sit down for the weeds.

Anon

The Bottle of Perfume

The bottle of perfume that Willie sent
Was highly displeasing to Millicent;
    Her thanks were so cold,
    They quarrelled, I'm told,
Through that silly scent Willie sent
    Millicent.

Anon

Lark

Hear
That lark
Bold and clear
Far over the park
Rising slowly into the sky,
Joy of morning in his throat,
Until he becomes a dot on high,
A distant speck of sound, a throbbing note,
Companion of the noonday sun, nearly a thousand feet
Above the rooftops, and there he hovers in the haze,
The air his shining kingdom and the clouds his chosen seat.
And then at last contented with his song of praise,
He drops to earth as if on failing wings;
Before on quiet ground he gently touches down.
I'll not forget the song he sings
Over the houses of the town;
Though I watch him disappear.
Still in the dark,
Bold and clear
That lark
Hear.

Leonard Clark

Ice in the Wind

Ice in the wind, storm-thrashed heather,
A voice, "Come in out of this wild weather."
A round stone hut on the empty moor,
A creaking hinge, an opening door.

Smoke from the fire, a low domed room,
A baby coughing, faces in the gloom,
Sparks at the hearth, a lifted brand,
A bowl that steamed in an outstretched
  hand.

I shook my head. I could not stay.
"I've lost the path." "Go west a way."
A nod, a smile, the door again,
Out into the dusk and the pelt of rain.

Ice in the wind, storm-thrashed heather,
No relief from the worsening weather,
Just bare hills and me, alone,
Standing by a heap of tumbled stone.

Richard Edwards

In the Misty, Murky Graveyard

In the misty, murky graveyard
   there's a midnight dance,
and in moonlight shaking skeletons
are twirling in a trance.
Linked bony arm in arm
they point and pitch and prance,
down there in the graveyard
   at the midnight dance.

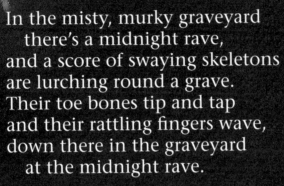

In the misty, murky graveyard
　　there's a midnight rave,
and a score of swaying skeletons
are lurching round a grave.
Their toe bones tip and tap
and their rattling fingers wave,
down there in the graveyard
　　at the midnight rave.

In the misty, murky graveyard
　　there's a midnight romp,
and a squad of skinless skeletons
all quiver as they stomp.
To the whistle of the wind
they clink and clank and clomp,
down there in the graveyard
　　at the midnight romp.

Wes Magee

15

Three Riddles

Head with a tail,
Each day plumper.
On the way
From jelly to jumper.

Case
For last place.

Space Vehicle:
One of a fleet of nine.
This one, though,
Is yours and mine.

Eric Finney

Three Riddles

Above the green carpet
The great fried egg
Sits in his blue bath.

Look at him nibbling the page
Leaving the blue behind,
How efficient he must be,
So thin and straight and tall,
And always on the ball.

Hundreds of stiff white legs
On one enormous neck
And all those legs let loose
Inside your open mouth.

George Szirtes

Ten Things Found in a Wizard's Pocket

A dark night.
Some words that nobody could ever spell.
A glass of water full to the top.
A large elephant.
A vest made from spiders' webs.
A handkerchief the size of a car park.
A bill from the wand shop.
A bucket full of stars and planets, to mix
    with the dark night.
A bag of magic mints you can suck for ever.
A snoring rabbit.

Ian McMillan

The Flower-Fed Buffaloes

The flower-fed buffaloes of the spring
In the days of long ago,
Ranged where the locomotives sing
And the prairie flowers lie low: –
The tossing, blooming, perfumed grass
Is swept away by the wheat,
Wheels and wheels and wheels spin by
In the spring that still is sweet.
But the flower-fed buffaloes of the spring
Left us, long ago.
They gore no more, they bellow no more,
they trundle the hills no more: –
With the Blackfeet, lying low,
With the Pawnees, lying low,
Lying low.

Vachel Lindsay

Sea Timeless Song

Hurricane come
and hurricane go
but sea ... sea timeless
sea timeless
sea timeless
sea timeless
sea timeless.

Hibiscus bloom
then dry-wither so
but sea ... sea timeless
sea timeless
sea timeless
sea timeless
sea timeless.

Tourist come
and tourist go
but sea ... sea timeless
sea timeless
sea timeless
sea timeless
sea timeless.

Grace Nichols

Sweet Chestnuts

How still the woods were! Not a redbreast whistled
    To mark the end of a mild autumn day.
    Under the trees the chestnut-cases lay,
Looking like small green hedgehogs softly bristled.

Plumply they lay, each with its fruit packed tight;
    For when we rolled them gently with our feet,
    The outer shells burst wide apart and split,
Showing the chestnuts brown and creamy-white.

Quickly we kindled a bright fire of wood,
    And placed them in the ashes. There we sat,
    Listening how all our chestnuts popped and spat.
And then, the smell how rich, the taste how good!

John Walsh

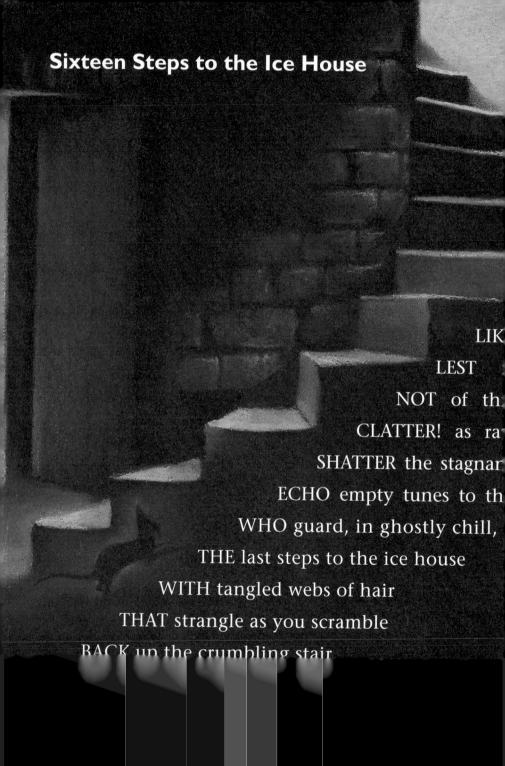

Sixteen Steps to the Ice House

LIK

LEST

NOT of th

CLATTER! as ra

SHATTER the stagnar

ECHO empty tunes to th

WHO guard, in ghostly chill,

THE last steps to the ice house

WITH tangled webs of hair

THAT strangle as you scramble

BACK up the crumbling stair

SIXTEEN steps to the ice house

BLACK with slime-slither mould,

SIXTEEN steps to the dungeon depths

AND that petrifying cold

HAT holds the souls of servants

eath afraid to breathe

sturbs some sinewy shape –

ntury.

attered bones

ill,

ead

Gina Douthwaite

Moon

(i)

bright still clean high
porthole in the morning sky

high clean still bright
space-explorer's traffic-light

still bright high clean
loop-the-lunar trampoline

clean high bright still
gift on morning's windowsill

(ii)

you
    spume-thrower
      wave-stretcher
        foam-snatcher
          spray-raiser
            surf-slinger
            string-puller
          scene-shifter
        tide-turner
      moon

Sue Cowling

Stopping by Woods on a Snowy Evening

Whose woods these are I think I know.
His house is in the village though;
He will not see me stopping here
To watch his woods fill up with snow.

My little horse must think it queer
To stop without a farmhouse near
Between the woods and frozen lake
The darkest evening of the year.

He gives his harness bells a shake
To ask if there is some mistake.
The only other sound's the sweep
Of easy wind and downy flake.

The woods are lovely, dark and deep.
But I have promises to keep,
And miles to go before I sleep,
And miles to go before I sleep.

Robert Frost

First Sight

Lambs that learn to walk in snow
When their bleating clouds the air
Meet a vast unwelcome, know
Nothing but a sunless glare.
Newly stumbling to and fro
All they find, outside the fold,
Is a wretched width of cold.

As they wait beside the ewe,
Her fleeces wetly caked, there lies
Hidden round them, waiting too,
Earth's immeasurable surprise.
They could not grasp it if they knew,
What so soon will wake and grow
Utterly unlike the snow.

Philip Larkin

Hiker's Haikus

i
This is the best way
To travel: on your two feet
Fuelled by bread and meat.

ii
On footpaths, through fields
Of daisies, cowslips, clear streams,
Alone with your dreams.

iii
Far from motorway's
Incessant roar, dust and stink –
Slow steps, time to think.

iv
Inhaling pure air
Seasoned with birdsong, green scent
No one could invent.

v
Quiet happiness,
Moving thoughtful, calm and slow;
The best way to go.

Vernon Scannell

Haiku

To convey one's mood
in seventeen syllables
is very diffic

John Cooper-Clarke

No!

No sun – no moon!
No morn – no noon –
No dawn – no dusk – no proper time of day –
No sky – no earthly view –
No distance looking blue –
No road – no street – no "t'other side the way" –
No top to any steeple –
No recognitions of familiar people
No courtesies for showing 'em –
No knowing 'em!
No travelling at all – no locomotion –
No inkling of the way – no notion –
"No go" – by land or ocean –
No mail – no post –
No news from any foreign coast –
No park – no ring – no afternoon gentility –
No company – no nobility –
No warmth, no cheerfulness, no healthful ease,
No comfortable feel in any member –
No shade, no shine, no butterflies, no bees,
No fruits, no flowers, no leaves, no birds.
November!

Thomas Hood

Winter Days

Biting air
Winds blow
City streets
Under snow

Noses red
Lips sore
Runny eyes
Hands raw

Chimneys smoke
Cars crawl
Piled snow
On garden wall

Slush in gutters
Ice in lanes
Frosty patterns
On window panes

Morning call
Lift up head
Nipped by winter
Stay in bed

Gareth Owen

Amulet

Inside the wolf's fang, the mountain of heather.
Inside the mountain of heather, the wolf's fur.
Inside the wolf's fur, the ragged forest.
Inside the ragged forest, the wolf's foot.
Inside the wolf's foot, the stony horizon.
Inside the stony horizon, the wolf's tongue.
Inside the wolf's tongue, the doe's tears.
Inside the doe's tears, the frozen swamp.
Inside the frozen swamp, the wolf's blood.
Inside the wolf's blood, the snow wind.
Inside the snow wind, the wolf's eye.
Inside the wolf's eye, the North star.
Inside the North star, the wolf's fang.

Ted Hughes

November Night

Listen ...
With faint dry sound,
Like steps of passing ghosts,
The leaves, frost-crisped, break from
    the trees
And fall.

Adelaide Crapsey

The Sands of Dee

"O Mary, go and call the cattle home,
    And call the cattle home,
    And call the cattle home,
    Across the sands of Dee";
The western wind was wild and dank with foam,
    And all alone went she.

The western tide crept up along the sand,
    And o'er and o'er the sand,
    And round and round the sand,
    As far as eye could see.
The rolling mist came down and hid the land:
    And never home came she.

"O is it weed, or fish, or floating hair –
    A tress of golden hair,
    A drownèd maiden's hair,
    Above the nets at sea?"
Was never salmon yet that shone so fair
    Among the stakes of Dee.

They rowed her in across the rolling foam,
    The cruel crawling foam,
    The cruel hungry foam,
    To her grave beside the sea:
But still the boatmen hear her call the cattle home
    Across the sands of Dee.

Charles Kingsley

The Eagle

He clasps the crag with crooked hands;
Close to the sun in lonely lands,
Ring'd with the azure world, he stands.

The wrinkled sea beneath him crawls;
He watches from his mountain walls,
And like a thunderbolt he falls.

Alfred, Lord Tennyson

Ozymandias

I met a traveller from an antique land
Who said: Two vast and trunkless legs of
    stone
Stand in the desert ... Near them, on the
    sand,
Half sunk, a shattered visage lies, whose
    frown,
And wrinkled lip, and sneer of cold
    command,
Tell that its sculptor well those passions
    read
Which yet survive, stamped on these
    lifeless things,
The hand that mocked them, and the heart
    that fed:
And on the pedestal these words appear:
'My name is Ozymandias, king of kings:
Look on my works, ye Mighty and despair!'
Nothing beside remains. Round the decay
Of that colossal wreck, boundless and bare
The lone and level sands stretch far away.

Percy Bysshe Shelley

Happy Birthday from Bennigans

Why did you do it, Mother?
I told you – didn't I – that I'd go with you
to a restaurant for my birthday
on one condition: Don't go and blab
to the waitress it's my BIG DAY.
But you had to go and tell her.
God, what if somebody had seen me?
I realise that you and Daddy
simply do not care if you ruin my reputation.
I almost thought for a teensy second
you had restrained yourself for once.
But no. You and your big mouth.
"Hip, hop, happy, b, birth, day,
hap, hap, happy, Happy Birthday to You!":
a zero girl, singing a zero song
at the top of her nothingness of a voice.
"All of us at Bennigans hope it's a
    special day!"
All of them, Mother, not just some.
That's IT for birthdays from now on.
Next year I'll be celebrating by myself.

Julie O'Callaghan

An Attempt at Unrhymed Verse

People tell you all the time,
Poems do not have to rhyme.
It's often better if they don't
And I'm determined this one won't.
   Oh dear.

Never mind, I'll start again,
Busy, busy with my pen … cil.
I can do it, if I try –
Easy, peasy, pudding and gherkins.

Writing verse is so much fun,
Cheering as the summer weather,
Makes you feel alert and bright,
'Specially when you get it more or less
   the way you want it.

Wendy Cope

As, as, as ...

As slow as a start
as stopped as a heart
as thin as a chip
as chapped as a lip
as dour as a door
as high as the floor
as far as away
as near as today
as dreamy as far
as tall as a star
as dark as a lock
as stopped as a clock
as slow as a hiss
as near as a miss

as slim as an 'i'
as puzzled as 'y'
as warm as a purr
as boring as sir
as boring as sir
as boring as sir
as scrunched as a list
as white as a fist
as bold as a blizzard
as old as a wizard
as sad as the sea
as fit as a flea
as sick as our cat
as yukky as that
as slow as an end
as there as a friend
as quick as a kiss
as finished as this.

Robert Hull

One Girl to Nil

ONE GIRL
TO NIL

Whacker Zach zipped up the pitch,
drew up sharply with a stitch,
disappeared beneath a 'scrum'.
Scarce of air he went quite numb.
To the rescue came young Zeph
like the west wind, from the left,
wafted on in borrowed kit –
burst the blighters like a zit.

•

Studded boots mashed blood with mud,
heads met others with a thud.
Zephyr sent their senses crashing,
scored a winner bully bashing,
dribbled off towards the goal,
wobbling like a new-born foal,
wumphed the ball – her final kill.
Zach's team won:

ONE GIRL
TO NIL

Gina Douthwaite

Requiem

(This is the epitaph on Robert Louis Stevenson's tomb on a hill-top in Samoa.)

Under the wide and starry sky
Dig the grave and let me lie.
Glad did I live and gladly die
And I laid me down with a will.

This be the verse you grave for me:
'Here he lies where he longed to be;
Home is the sailor, home from sea,
And the hunter home from the hill'.

Robert Louis Stevenson